pocket posh® tips for knitters

Jayne Davis
and
Jodie Davis

Andrews McMeel
Publishing, LLC
Kansas City • Sydney • London

POCKET POSH® TIPS FOR KNITTERS

Andrews McMeel Publishing, LLC
an Andrews McMeel Universal company
1130 Walnut Street, Kansas City, Missouri 64106

www.andrewsmcmeel.com

11 12 13 14 15 SHZ 10 9 8 7 6 5 4 3 2 1

ISBN: 978-1-4494-0343-0

Library of Congress Control Number: 2010937876

Hand drawings by Iia Owens-Williams

Cover and interior knitwear by Shetland Collection
www.shetland-knitwear.co.uk

ATTENTION: SCHOOLS AND BUSINESSES

Andrews McMeel books are available at quantity discounts with
bulk purchase for educational, business, or sales promotional use.
For information, please e-mail the Andrews McMeel Publishing
Special Sales Department: specialsales@amuniversal.com

acknowledgments

How do you collect a book full of tips on knitting? You ask for them, and so we did. Countless e-mails went out to knit shop owners, knitting designers, and yarn companies all over the country asking for their favorite tips. A huge "Thank You" to each and every one who responded. This book wouldn't have been possible without you. Tips we've gleaned over the years listening to good knitting advice and ideas are included, too. And thanks to all of you who share this love of knitting.

contents

introduction

At the dawn of civilization, or probably before, someone discovered that if you twisted pieces of animal hair or plant fibers together you made a kind of yarn, and if you looped one loop into another they held together, and if you did that enough times you had something useful, and then someone discovered that using sticks made the whole process easier. And thus the art of what we call knitting developed through time. At different times and different places, different ways were found to accomplish the same things. And guess what: Each way is the right way. There is no absolutely right way to knit.

Today you can buy a perfectly good sweater for a low price. So why do we knit? Because we love it. We love the camaraderie of friends whose bond is this love affair with yarn. We knit to warm or adorn our family and friends, we knit for those we've never met and never will, but our hearts travel with each finished piece. We knit useful objects and others not so useful just for the fun of it. We join in spirit those who tend their flocks and grow the fibers, the spinners and dyers and those who stock their shelves with skeins of beauty. It's the touch and the texture of these glorious yarns and the colors—it's always about the colors.

We're thankful to be part of this passionate and diverse worldwide community of knitters and know you are thankful, too. We hope you enjoy this collection and discover some tips that will give you an "aha" moment that makes your knitting faster or easier and more fun.

Jayne and Jodie

it's all about the yarn

yarn

it's all about the yarn

I like making a piece of string into something
I can wear.
— Anonymous

Make sure to keep up with yarn companies whose products you like by registering on their Web sites. Make sure to do the same for the yarn stores you enjoy working with. We all work together, and it is important to be a part of your knitting family.

Barry Klein
Trendsetter Yarns
trendsetteryarns.com

....

In knitting, as in life, I believe it is always important to have a lifeline. When I'm working on a complex pattern or working with super-fussy yarns, I run a piece of waste yarn along with one row of knitting. I may add a new one every few inches or further, if I am feeling particularly confident. If I make a mistake or drop a stitch, I can easily frog to my lifeline: the last place I knew my work was perfect. It makes it so much easier to pick up the stitches and correct the mistakes.

Jonelle Beck
SWTC, Inc.
soysilk.com

....

When choosing spaced dyed yarns for a project, if you want a striped look, choose a yarn that has colors with different or contrasting values; if you don't want prominent stripes, choose a yarn with colors of equal or similar values.

Laura Schickli
Handwerks
handwerkstextiles.com

....

Intarsia Untangled: If your intarsia project includes a lot of color changes and you find the dangling bobbins frustrating, here is another method of taming the tangles. Line up the yarns you will be using in a shallow cardboard box and cut slits on the side of the box for the yarns to come through (Fig. 1). As you work the first row, flip your work as you turn it, and you'll find the yarns will uncross themselves as you knit across.

At the end of the second row your yarns are all uncrossed. Not easy for traveling but great when knitting in your favorite chair at home.

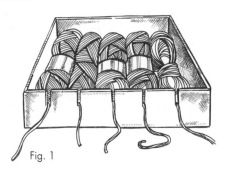

Fig. 1

When substituting a yarn of similar gauge, purchase yarn by yardage, not weight. For example, acrylic weighs less than cotton, and you will need more grams of a cotton yarn when substituting it for an acrylic or acrylic-blend yarn. Look up the yardage of the recommended yarn and multiply by the number of skeins called for in the pattern. This is how many yards of the substitute yarn you will need to buy. Yarndex is an excellent resource for both yardage and weight of most commercial yarns.

Kay Mather
Rare Purls
rarepurls.net

Can I combine two strands of one-weight yarn to equal a larger weight? The following are approximate equivalents. You should always create a swatch to be sure you are obtaining the gauge needed.

- 2 strands fingering = one strand sport.
- 2 strands sport = one strand worsted.
- 2 strands worsted = one strand super bulky.

Editors at Lion Brand Yarn
lionbrandyarn.com

....

If you use hand-dyed yarn, be sure to get enough yarn to complete your project since each bag could be a different dye lot, and skeins may vary from bag to bag.

Malabrigo Yarn
malabrigoyarn.com

....

If you run out of yarn and can't buy the same dye lot, try blending the dye lots. Work a couple rows alternating each of the yarns to blend them. If you have completed large sections, you might have to frog some of it back and do the blending just so that the transition is nice.

Linda Lum DeBono
lindalumdebono.com

It is often difficult to calculate the amount of yarn needed for a long tail cast on. The usual method is to loosely wrap the yarn around the needle, but this is often too long or too short. I now make a slip knot using a strand of yarn from each end of the skein. When I am finished casting on I snip one of the ends, leaving a tail long enough to weave into my work.

Elaine Glazer
Dogs n Roses

. . . .

Love the yarn you are working with. There is nothing better than enjoying every stitch you make.

. . . .

Don't overthink your projects. Simple knitting with an exotic yarn can lead to a magical and priceless piece that you will cherish forever.

Nadine Curtis
Be Sweet
besweetyarns.com

. . . .

Choosing 100 percent natural, organic yarns in natural colors demonstrates your care for the earth, and your creation can be returned to the earth at the end of its useful

7

life as compost. Perhaps someday your granddaughter will eat a cucumber grown in compost from the sweater you are knitting for your daughter today. Consider the new soft cotton yarns that are hybridized to produce pretty pastels without dyeing, for example. Have a green one!

Leslie Willoughby
The Green Thread
GreenThreadWorld.com

Recycling Yarn: Do you have a hand-knitted sweater that is totally out of style or no longer fits, but you love the yarn? Recycle it! Carefully unravel the yarn and loosely wrap it

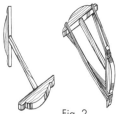

into skeins. To skein, use a niddy noddy (Fig. 2), a swift, two chairs turned back to back, or anything you can loop the yarn around. Tie each skein in four places and then soak the skeins in warm, soapy water. Be sure not to agitate, as you don't want the yarn to felt if it's wool. Rinse the

Fig. 2

skeins thoroughly and hang to dry. When dry, wind into balls, and your yarn is ready to knit another day.

Kirstin Muench
Muench Yarns, Inc.
muenchyarns.com

Yarn Control: Nothing is more annoying than having your ball of working yarn rolling all over the floor, especially if you have animals that shed or like to chase the ball. Here are some simple tips to keep your yarn close at hand and clean.

Easiest of all is to put the ball in a small or medium-size deep, heavy ceramic or stoneware bowl. Also available from some ceramic shops are "yarn bowls," hand turned with various slits or holes to keep the yarn from jumping out of the bowl.

Two-liter plastic drink bottles make good yarn caddies. Cut a hole in the side of a clean bottle large enough to squeeze a ball of yarn through. Slip the loose end of the yarn through the bottle neck. A half-gallon milk bottle works equally well, and it has a handle.

In fact, any container that is large enough and has a removable lid will work just fine. Look in your kitchen, pantry, and recycling bin. An oatmeal container works. Just poke a small hole in the plastic lid to slip the yarn end through. (Make sure you smooth off any rough edges.) An empty baby wipe container fits the bill. There's no end to the possibilities. You can dress up your yarn holder with craft paints, fabric, and yarns to make it your own.

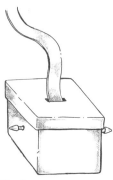

Here's a way to keep ribbon yarn from twisting as it's used. Find a box the spool of ribbon will fit inside. Cut a slit in the center of the lid for the ribbon to slip through. Poke a hole in the center of two opposite sides of the box. Slide a double-pointed needle through one hole, slip the ribbon spool onto the needle, and then slide through the opposite hole. Place a needle protector on each end of the needle to keep it from slipping out. Thread the end of the ribbon through the slit in the lid and replace (Fig. 3). The spool stays put, and the ribbon won't twist.

Fig. 3

Most of us knitters can't resist buying more beautiful yarn, and we end up with a large stash. How to keep track of what we have without pulling out the entire collection and sorting through? Inventory control. Here's one simple method. Keep a record on index cards and store them in a recipe card box. Staple the label from one skein onto a card (Fig. 4). Record the number of balls and total yardage (yardage marked on label × number of balls) and suggested needle size. Punch a hole in the upper right corner and tie on a 6" sample of the yarn. Next time you have a pattern you'd like to knit, shop from your stash before you head to your local yarn shop. These cards are also handy when you'd like to find a blending yarn or fabric. Just take the card shopping with you.

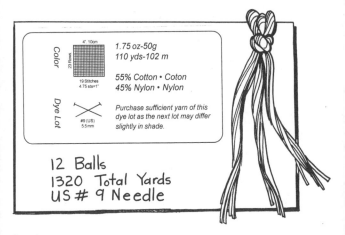

Color

4". 10cm

23 Rows

19 Stitches
4.75 sts=1"

1.75 oz-50g
110 yds-102 m

55% Cotton • Coton
45% Nylon • Nylon

Dye Lot

#9 (US)
5.5 mm

Purchase sufficient yarn of this dye lot as the next lot may differ slightly in shade.

12 Balls
1320 Total Yards
US # 9 Needle

Fig. 4

To Wind a Center-Pull Ball of Yarn

1. Grasp yarn tail between thumb and index finger, letting a 9-inch tail hang across your palm (Fig. 5).

2. Bring the working yarn behind index finger and wrap around the thumb, index, and middle fingers. Wrap twelve times, making sure the tail remains free (Fig. 6).

3. Remove the wraps from your fingers, hold horizontally, and wrap the working yarn around the center six times (Fig. 7).

4. Turn the bundle so that the center wrap is horizontal and the working yarn comes forward (Fig. 8).

5. Make sure the tail hangs down freely. Then begin wrapping a ball around the bundle, starting at the center wraps. Bring yarn from bottom right side diagonally up to the left side and around. Shift the bundle a quarter turn clockwise every five wraps so they will be evenly distributed around the ball (Fig. 9).

6. Continue until all the yarn is used up. Pull on the tail to release the yarn from the center of the ball (Fig. 10).

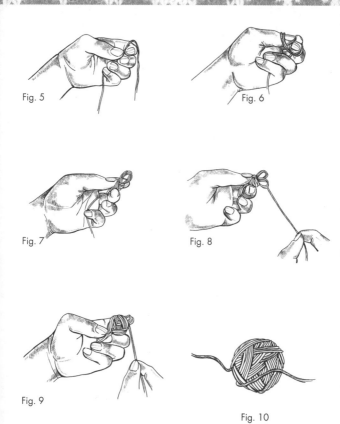

Fig. 5

Fig. 6

Fig. 7

Fig. 8

Fig. 9

Fig. 10

A yarn butterfly is used whenever you need small lengths of yarn, such as for argyle knitting. The butterfly is a small center-pull skein that keeps the yarn out of your way when it's not in use. To make, place the yarn around your thumb so that the end dangles in your palm. Then wind the yarn you'll need in a figure eight between your thumb and little finger (Fig. 11). To secure the butterfly, tie the final end around the center of the bundle in two or three half hitches. Knit from the end of yarn that dangled in your palm. If the butterfly loosens too much as you use the yarn, retie the half hitches.

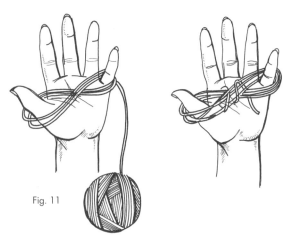

Fig. 11

Make your own yarn bobbins by cutting the pattern (Fig. 13) from old plastic food storage containers. Trace the pattern onto the plastic, cut out, and smooth the edges. Perfect!

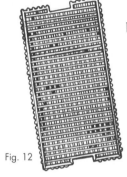

Another way to make your own bobbins is to cut them from plastic needlepoint canvas. Cut a 2 × 4-inch piece for each bobbin. Cut out some squares at the top and bottom as shown on the pattern (Fig. 12), trim off the corners, and cut slits halfway down each side to anchor the yarn.

Fig. 12

If you need to divide a ball of yarn in two equal parts, weigh the ball on a digital scale. Divide that weight in half and then start winding off yarn and weighing the new ball from time to time. When it equals the desired amount, cut the yarn, and you have two equal balls.

The label tells you the story of your yarn.

Fig. 13

how much yarn do i need?

how much yarn do i need?

If you give a friend a scarf, she'll have an accessory. If you teach her to knit, she'll be in stitches the rest of her life.
— *Anonymous*

This chart estimates how much yarn you will need for specific crafts.

	Knit Yardage		Crochet Yardage	
AFGHAN	Baby 20" x 30"	Adult 60" x 60"	Baby 20" x 30"	Adult 60" x 60"
Lace, sock, or fingering	1,351	3,500	1,760	4,500
Sport/DK	1,150	2,950	1,500	3,835
Worsted	1,000	2,660	1,300	3,450
Chunky or bulky	850	1,875	1,100	2,500

	Knit Yardage		Crochet Yardage	
HAT	Child (head size) 18″	Adult (head size) 20″–22″	Child (head size) 18″	Adult (head size) 20″–22″
Sport/DK	175	225–275	230	230–360
Worsted	175	225–250	230	230–360
Chunky or bulky	125	150–175	162	195–210
SCARF	Child 6″ × 40″	Adult 8″ × 54″	Child 6″ × 40″	Adult 8″ × 54″
Lace, sock, or fingering	440	660	572	860
Sport/DK	350	650	455	845
Worsted	190	380	247	495
Chunky or bulky	125	250	163	325

	Knit Yardage		Crochet Yardage	
SWEATER	Child (chest size) 24"/28"/ 32"	Adult (chest size) 36"/40"/ 44"/48"	Child (chest size) 24"/28"/ 32"	Adult (chest size) 36"/40"/ 44"/48"
Lace, sock, or fingering	750/ 1,000/ 1,450	1,800/ 2,100/ 2,500/ 2,700	675/ 1,300/ 1,885	2,340/ 2,730/ 3,250/ 3,510
Sport/DK	550/ 800/ 1,100	1,400/ 1,600/ 1,900/ 2,100	715/ 1,040/ 1,430	1,820/ 2,080/ 2,470/ 2,730
Worsted	500/ 650/ 1,000	1,200/ 1,400/ 1,600/ 1,800	650/ 845/ 1,300	1,560/ 1,820/ 2,080/ 2,340
Chunky or bulky	350/ 500/ 700	900/ 1,000/ 1,200/ 1,300	360/ 650/ 910	1,170/ 1,300/ 1,560/ 1,690

	Knit Yardage		Crochet Yardage	
VEST	Child (chest size) 24"/ 28"/ 32"	Adult (chest size) 36"/ 40"/ 44"/ 48"	Child (chest size) 24"/ 28"/ 32"	Adult (chest size) 36"/ 40"/ 44"/ 48"
Lace, sock, or fingering	400/ 550/ 750	950/ 1,125/ 1,300/ 1,450	520/ 715/ 975	1,235/ 1,465/ 1,642/ 1,885
Sport/DK	300/ 400/ 600	700/ 850/ 950/ 1,100	390/ 520/ 780	910/ 1,175/ 1,235/ 1,430
Worsted	250/ 350/ 500	600/ 750/ 850/ 950	325/ 455/ 650	780/ 975/ 1,105/ 1,235

	Knit Yardage		Crochet Yardage	
Chunky or bulky	175/ 250/ 400	450/ 550/ 650/ 700	228/ 325/ 520	585/ 715/ 845/ 910

*NOTE: Amounts are only approximate, based on average-size projects, and will vary depending on type of stitch, gauge, and differences in individual knitters and crocheters. To find out how many skeins, balls, or cones to purchase, divide the total yardage needed by the chosen yarn's amount per skein, ball, or cone. Be sure to round up to the nearest whole skein, ball, or cone. For example, to make an adult afghan out of Homespun® you will need 1,875 yards of yarn. Each skein of Homespun® contains 185 yards, so you will need eleven skeins of yarn.

The Editors at Lion Brand Yarn
lionbrandyarn.com

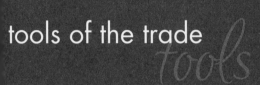

tools of the trade

tools of the trade

*There will always be knitting as long as there
are two sticks and a string.*
—*Anonymous*

Coil-type wraps are a great way to keep your needles together when not knitting. These are small, stretchy coils that wrap around the shafts of your needles to prevent stitches from sliding off. Usually the coils come in sizes that match your needle gauge. To keep from losing them while you are knitting, attach a safety pin-type marker to your work (Fig. 14). When you take the wrap off your needles, attach it to the locking stitch marker, and you will not lose it while knitting (Fig. 15). Wrap one of these nonslip coils around both ends of your double points when you've finished knitting, and your work will not slip off the needles.

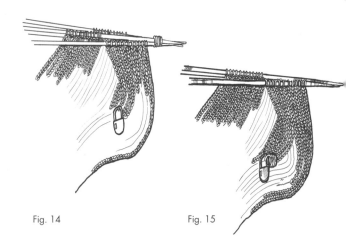

Fig. 14   Fig. 15

Use point protectors. Knitting needle point protectors fit on the tips of your needles and are generally used for preventing needle breakage; however, they can also be effective at keeping stitches in place.

Use a needle holder. Double-pointed needle holders help sock and lace knitters keep stitches in place. These are generally small cylinders that hold needles and have a slot on one side for allowing knitted fabric to hang free.

Painter's tape (the blue stuff) is a great alternative to highlighter tape or sticky notes for marking your place on a pattern. It adheres better than either of the other methods.

As a person new to lacework in shawls, I have found stitch markers to be very valuable. However, in my first triangular shawl, I still had problems with my count because I inadvertently counted the same side twice. Now I have a new technique: I use a different color marker on each side. If my pattern or stitch count is off, I can remember that it was one way on the green side, for instance, and another count on the purple side. Color coding has helped me keep it straight and catch mistakes easily.

Barbara Pinto
New York City, NY

....

When using circular needles that still have some curl in them, place them in a sink or basin of warm water to straighten them. This makes them much easier to work with.

John Little
Briggs and Little
briggsandlittle.com

....

I almost always use circular needles. They are much more convenient than the conventional pairs of straight knitting needles even for flat knitting. When you are making garments in one piece, the knitting can get very heavy. With straight knitting needles this weight is supported by your arms;

29

with circular needles it rests much more comfortably in your lap. Circular needles can also hold far more stitches than straight needles.

Brandon Mably
Brandon Mably Design
brandonmably.com

The use of circular needles has many benefits. They are not only for knitting in the round but also for projects that require extra needle length. They are also great for things like picking up stitches around an armhole or edge where flexibility is essential. The circular needle also is better for your wrists if you suffer from carpal tunnel syndrome as it eases the strain on your wrists. It is also the needle of choice for airplane travel: It's easy to carry, and it keeps your work in your lap rather than your neighbor's.

Mary Bonnette
The Sassy Skein
sassyskein.com

What in the world is this (Fig. 16)? It's a nostepinne, a Scandinavian carved wooden knitting tool used to wind a center-pull ball of yarn the old-fashioned, low-tech way. A "nosty" is virtually unbreakable, completely portable, doesn't require clamping to a table, and needs no batteries. Google *nostepinne* on your computer and you'll find several video instructions and vendors where you can buy one of your very own.

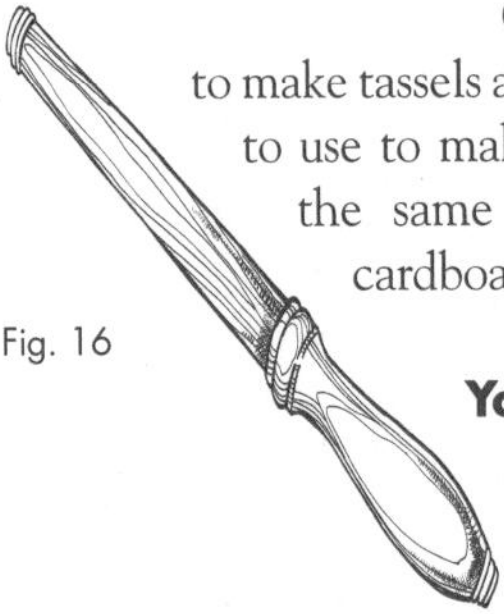

Gadgets abound. There are tools to make tassels and pom-poms and fringe that are fun to use to make trims for our projects. Of course, the same thing can be accomplished with cardboard cut to the needed size.

Fig. 16

You should have a knitting bag. There are all sorts of choices, ranging from the absolute beauties at your local yarn shop to a canvas bag pulled off your closet shelf (you know you have a few stashed away). Some people like to use a good-sized basket with a handle. Please don't use a paper shopping bag; you'll be really annoyed when it splits and everything spills on the floor.

Here are some suggestions for the contents. Store all the following small pieces in a small zipper bag and drop it in the knitting bag. There are plenty on the market, but a cosmetic bag or even a quart-size zippered plastic food bag works well.

1. **Tape measure:** You'll always want to measure your work in progress. Either a dressmaker's tape or a

retractable will do. Just be sure it's made of a non-stretchable material, but not metal.

2. **Stitch holders:** There are all kinds of these on the market. It doesn't make any difference which type you choose, but be sure to have at least two in various lengths.

3. **Row counters:** One type slips on your needle, and you turn the counter as you finish each row. They come in two sizes to fit on both small gauge needles and larger needles. You'll need both sizes. There's also a small freestanding counter on the market that works well.

4. **Stitch markers:** These are small circles of metal or plastic that come in various sizes. They slip on your needle to mark a change in the pattern or on circular needles to mark the beginning of a new row.

5. **Locking stitch markers:** These markers can be easily placed anywhere and removed whenever you want.

6. **Scissors:** A small pair of sharp embroidery scissors works just fine. You'll always have something that needs cutting.

7. **Yarn needle:** These come in both plastic and metal. Have a couple in case one gets misplaced.

8. **Needle protectors:** These are made of plastic or rubber and fit on the ends of your needles. They protect your needle points when not in use and also keep your stitches from slipping off the needles. They come in two sizes, and you should have both sizes.

9. **Coil wraps:** These are nonslip coils that wrap around the ends of your needles to hold them together. They'll also keep stitches from sliding off the needles.

10. **Small pad and pencil:** You never know when you'll wish you had them.

11. **Crochet hook:** Keep a small hook size D or E on hand. This is very handy for fixing dropped stitches.

12. **Cable needles:** Have two different sizes in your bag.

13. **Needle gauge:** Over time the markings on wood and bamboo needles can rub away. A metal or plastic needle gauge will give you the correct size.

14. **Small glass fingernail file:** This is handy to use to smooth down any rough spots that pop up on a needle.

15. **Small container of greaseless hand cream.**

16. **Copy of this book.**

17. **Photocopy of your pattern** slipped into a plastic sheet protector.

18. **Gauge sample** slipped into the same sheet protector.

19. **Working project** in a portable bag. This can be as simple as a gallon-size zippered plastic bag or a fabric drawstring or zippered bag large enough to hold the project.

20. **One or two balls** of the project yarn.

21. **Extra needle in the same size** as the project working needles. This covers the emergency if you should lose or break a needle.

22. **Crochet hook in the same diameter** as the project knitting needles.

23. **An extra project all bagged** and ready to go just in case you have room in your knitting bag.

Here are a few "in a pinch" substitutes.

Stitch markers: safety pins, scrap yarn in loop ties, rubber bands, garbage bag ties, costume jewelry rings, or loop earrings.

Cable needle: bent paperclip, plastic-covered electrical wire.

Needle alternates: fast-food chopsticks (preferably new), bamboo skewers, pencils, ballpoint pens.

Skein holder: back of dining room chair or other piece of furniture, or hands of significant other or wayward child.

Ruler: The length of an American dollar bill is 6 inches.

Yarn ball container: shoe, empty and clean plastic milk jug (cut a flap in one side large enough to insert ball, then pull thread end through pour spout), or a mixing bowl covered with punctured plastic wrap.

Containment of slippery yarns: Put ball in knee-high stocking.

why swatch?

why swatch?

why swatch?

> *Really, all you need to become a good knitter are wool, needles, hands and a slightly below average intelligence. Of course, superior intelligence, such as yours and mine, is an advantage.*
> —Elizabeth Zimmerman

Always do your gauge swatch. Most people like to avoid this, or they say, "I'm always on gauge." I always say, "If you don't do your gauge, you deserve what you get when it doesn't fit." Make a swatch as written in the pattern or on the label and add extra stitches. Measure across the swatch and get an average rather than measuring just 1 inch.

Don't rip out your swatch. Keep it in case you need more yarn. Also, wash your swatch, block your swatch. Test that swatch in every way so you know what will happen with the finished knit piece.

Barry Klein
Trendsetter Yarns
trendsetteryarns.com

All too often I hear knitters say they do not knit a gauge swatch because they always knit to the recommended gauge. Whoa! That recommended gauge comes from a sample knitter, and sample knitters vary from pattern to pattern. Without a gauge swatch, you are leaving the finished size of your project to "by guess and by golly."

Kay Mather
Rare Purls
rarepurls.net

I sympathize with knitters who want to get on with the job and do not want to spend time on gauge samples. However, the same instructions in the hands of tight or loose knitters can end up in a child's jacket or a huge coat. So the dreaded gauge squares are absolutely essential if hours of work are not to be wasted.

Brandon Mably
Brandon Mably Design
brandonmably.com

How do I know which yarn to use for a project I want to make? The gauge of your pattern determines which weight of yarn you should select. You can use any yarn that has a suggested gauge equal to the gauge of your pattern. You can generally substitute one yarn in a weight class for another.

WHY SWATCH?

In all cases, be sure to swatch and check your gauge carefully, using whatever size hook or needle is needed to obtain the gauge of the pattern. This method works best if the gauge of your pattern is given over stockinettete if knitting, or over single crochet if crocheting. Be sure you are satisfied with the fabric that results; it should be neither too stiff nor too loose. Be aware that since you are using a different yarn, your project will not look exactly the same as that pictured with the pattern.

Editors at Lion Brand Yarn
lionbrandyarn.com

If you are not getting the suggested gauge, do not try knitting tighter or more loosely. Change the size of the needle you are using. Think of a golfer. In golf, a player keeps his or her natural, unique swing for every drive, changing clubs to make shots of different lengths. Use the natural tension you have developed as a knitter and change needle size to alter your gauge.

Kay Mather
Rare Purls
rarepurls.net

41

Did you know that your gauge will probably be different when you are knitting in the round than when you are knitting flat? If your project is knit in the round, knit your gauge swatch in the round rather than back and forth. Use a 12-inch circular needle or knit the swatch over three needles, as in sock knitting.

Always, always, always knit a gauge swatch. This is the secret to a properly fitted garment. Even if your project is a scarf or blanket that doesn't need fitting, the swatch will help you obtain the proper gauge, giving you the results the pattern shows. Most of us are anxious to get started on our project; however, the time spent knitting a swatch can save you lots of heartache. Here are tips to knitting your swatch.

1. Always use the same needles you'll be using in the project. Needles of the same size in different materials can give you different results.

2. Knit a 5 × 5-inch swatch. Cast on the proper number of stitches (stitches per inch from the gauge listed in the pattern times 5) and knit for 5 inches using the pattern stitch. The gauge listed in most pattern instructions is for the predominant stitch pattern used in the design. If you're using a pattern stitch, cast on enough stitches for at least two pattern repeats.

3. Roughly measure after a couple of inches, and if it's too tight (too many stitches per inch) switch to a larger needle and if too loose (too few stitches per inch) switch to a smaller needle. Place a locking stitch marker at the end of the row so you'll know where you changed needle size.

4. Bind off after 5 inches. The gauge in most patterns is measured after blocking, so block your swatch using the same method you'll use with the project.

5. Lay the swatch on a table or countertop. Place a ruler straight across in the center of the swatch, count the number of stitches in 4 inches, and divide by four. This gives you the gauge per inch. Measure rows by placing the ruler vertically and count the number of rows in a 4-inch column.

6. If you're to gauge, congratulations; pass Go and start your project. If not, sorry, knit another swatch. You'll thank us later.

a good stitch

a good stitch

a good stitch

If I stitch fast enough, does it count as aerobic exercise?
— *Anonymous*

Here are two methods to eliminate the dreaded "jog" when knitting in solid stripes in the round.

1. When knitting circular stripes of two or more rounds:

   a. Knit a complete round in the new color.

   b. With the first stitch on the left needle, lift the right side of the stitch in the row below (a contrast color), place it on the left needle, and knit two together.

   c. The contrast color obliterates the new color and changes the location of the "first stitch." Move your beginning-round marker one stitch to the left and

continue with the new color for as many rounds as
you wish.

d. This stitch is worked only at the end of the first round
of a new color.

2. If you are knitting single-round stripes (e.g., one round of
red, one round of white), at the end of each round, pick
up each new color over the old, the opposite of intarsia.

Meg Swansen
Schoolhouse Press
Pittsville, Wisconsin
schoolhousepress.com

Here's a tip that's not well known. SSK (slip as if to knit,
slip as if to knit, place both stitches back on left-hand needle
and knit together through the back) produces a decrease that
slants in the opposite direction from knit two together. It
never looks quite as neat; often the first stitch, which reads as
on top, becomes slightly larger. During the action of knitting
two together, the tip of the right needle goes first through the
second stitch and then through the first stitch (placing the
second stitch on top when finished), and the stitch is usually
completed on the tips of the needle, making a neat decrease.
During SSK, it is very easy to put the entire needle through
the two stitches; because the first stitch winds up on top, it gets

distorted. The answer is to work SSKs on the very tips of the
needles, taking care that the full portion of the needle doesn't
slide all the way in.

Laura Bryant
Prism Arts, Inc.
prismyarn.com

....

For smooth edges on your knitting, always knit the first stitch
of a row and purl the last stitch of the row, no matter what
your pattern says.

Bebby Weigand
Delray Beach, Florida

....

I knit in all the ends of yarn as I work. This saves hours
of laborious darning in after the knitting is over. What you
do is this: When joining in a new yarn, leave ends of about
3 inches on the old yarn and the new; work the next two
stitches with the new yarn, then, holding both ends in your
left hand, lay them over the working yarn and work the next
stitch; now insert the right-hand needle into the next stitch
in the usual way, then bring the ends (still holding them in
your left hand) up over the point of the right-hand needle and
work this stitch past the ends. Carry on in this way, laying the
ends over the working yarns on every second or third stitch

and knitting past the ends on the following stitch until they are completely knitted in.

Brandon Mably
Brandon Mably Design
brandonmably.com

Grafting mantra: I do a lot of grafting: top to top, top to bottom, stockinettete to stockinettete, reverse stockinettete to reverse stockinettete, and even rib to rib. There's one rule that holds true in every one of these situations. It doesn't matter whether you knit continental or combination, and it doesn't matter which way the stitches are twisted on the needle. Always:

Use the front door (the knit side) when going across the street (to the next row).

Use the back door (the purl side) when going next door (to the next stitch).

1. To start a graft, with a long tail of yarn threaded through a tapestry needle, insert the needle into the purl side (and thus out the knit side) of the first stitch, the one the yarn is coming off from.

2. Cross to the other row, enter the first stitch through the knit side (front door) and thus out the back, and enter the second stitch through the purl side (back door) and thus out the front.

3. *Cross to the other row, enter the first stitch through the knit side, enter the second stitch through the purl side, and remove the first stitch from the needle.

4. Repeat from *.

Note: If there is a knit stitch followed by a purl stitch (in the same row), the yarn will need to go from the back of the fabric to the front of the fabric in following the back door rule.

That's all there is to it. Follow this simple rule and you may actually find that you enjoy grafting!

> *Carol Sunday Designs*
> *Sunday Knits Yarns*
> sundayknits.com

....

The two most common ways to decrease the number of stitches in knitting are slip, slip, knit (SSK) and purl two together. When the SSK is worked on the right side of the fabric, the SSK decrease slants to the left. To work, slip two stitches one at a time as if to knit. Insert the left needle into these two stitches from left to right (Fig. 17) and knit them together.

Kirstin Muench
Muench Yarns, Inc.
muenchyarns.com.

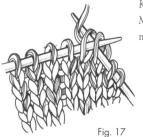

Fig. 17

If you have to start with a small number of stitches and then increase, or if you have to decrease to a small amount of stitches, and you need to work around on those stitches, instead of splitting them onto separate double-pointed needles, just work the stitches as you would I-cord until the rows are complete.

Lynne Lounsbury
Keepsake Quilting
keepsakequilting.com

After binding off in the round, instead of pulling the yarn through the last stitch loop, pull out the last loop and connect

the tail to the next stitch in the round using a darning needle.
This method will make a smoother edge.

Laura Schickli
Handwerks
handwerkstextiles.com

. . . .

Some cable charts appear quite busy, and it can be a slow
process to figure out which cable symbol you are seeing and
then locate it on the stitch key in order to knit it. Use colored
pencils and color each symbol in the key a different color, and
then color in the proper symbols on the chart. You will find it
much easier to pick out the proper cable cross you are to work.

Clara Masessa
Kraemer Yarns
kraemeryarns.com

. . . .

When you are casting on a lot of stitches using the long
tail cast-on method, use two balls of yarn. After the stitches
have been cast on, cut the yarn from one ball and continue
using the other for knitting. This takes away the guesswork of
how long the tail should be.

Black Sheep Knitting
Needham, Massachusetts
blacksheepknitting.com

Sometimes it's difficult to bind off a heavy or irregular yarn with a regular two-needle bind-off. Instead, substitute a crochet hook approximately the same diameter as the knitting needles. Put the hook through the first loop on the left-hand needle and knit the stitch onto the hook. Knit the next stitch onto the hook and pull the stitch through the first stitch on the hook (Fig. 18). Continue across the row to the end and pull the yarn through the last loop on the hook.

Kirstin Muench
Muench Yarns, Inc.
muenchyarns.com

Fig. 18

When casting on for a pair of socks, cast on the total number of stitches required on a straight needle of the correct size. Then transfer the stitches equally onto three double-pointed needles, and you're ready to begin knitting in the round. This eliminates the clumsiness of casting onto three separate needles.

Jean DeFrancis
Delray Beach, Florida

It took many years to learn that the cast on a right and wrong side and your cast-on should match up at the seams.

Ann Kelliher
Fancie Purls
Plymouth, Massachusetts
fanciepurls.vpweb.com

For years I did make 1 the way most directions say, by lifting the horizontal bar between stitches and knitting into the back, an awkward maneuver at best. Then I remembered doing something one time on a garment that wasn't called a make 1. Here's what you do: Where the directions say to do a make 1, just do a simple yarn over; on the next row, knit or purl into the back of the yarn over, which twists it just as if you had backward looped it in the first place. It's still a little awkward if you are purling that stitch, but if you are doing garter stitch so that the stitch is knit it is very easy.

99 percent of directions for SSK (left-leaning decrease) say to slip each of two stitches knitwise one at a time and then knit them together through the back loops. A better way is to slip the first stitch knitwise, but slip the second stitch purlwise, then knit two together through the back loops as before. Slipping the second stitch purlwise twists the stitch, but it lies underneath the first one anyway, so you don't see it. But because it is twisted it is a little tighter, and the double stitch lies a little flatter and smoother and more like a right-leaning knit two together.

Betty Balcomb
Bi Coastal Betty at Ravelry.com

....

For a closer-fitting glove, mitt, or sock, use a stitch pattern that has natural elasticity and cast on a couple of stitches less than your gauge indicates. Build in about 1/4- to 1/2-inch negative ease.

Laura Schickli
Handwerks
Handwerkstextiles.com

....

The three-needle bind-off makes a great shoulder seam, especially for children's garments. It is sturdy and secure without being bulky. In addition, if you are joining color work or a pattern stitch, your stitches line up exactly, giving your garment a very professional look.

Mary Bonnette
The Sassy Skein
sassyskein.com

....

Bead knitting is lots of fun and gives spectacular results. Here's a simple way to string beads on your yarn if you don't have a needle that will accommodate the yarn and also fit through the hole in the bead. Thread a sewing needle with a 10-inch length of regular sewing thread. Tie in a knot to make a circle. Slide the end of your yarn through the loop (Fig. 19). Thread several beads onto the needle and slide down onto the yarn (Fig. 20). Keep adding beads until you have the quantity needed. Watch the video on our Web site.

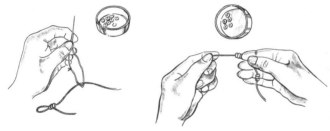

Fig. 19

Jimmy Beans Wool
jimmybeanswool.com

From time to time a pattern asks us to cast on stitches at the end of a row. Here's how. Insert your crochet hook in the edge stitch of the second row below your last stitch (Fig. 21) and draw up a loop. Make a loose chain in the number of stitches to be cast on (Fig. 22). Remove the crochet hook and insert the free knitting needle into the loop to make one stitch. Pick up and knit a loop in each remaining chain. When you come to the end of the chain, continue to knit across the row (Fig. 23). If you are working on a purl row, purl all the stitches.

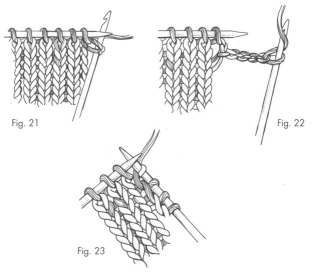

Fig. 21

Fig. 22

Fig. 23

The purl two together decrease slants to the right on the knit side of the fabric when it is worked on the purl side. To

purl two together, insert the right needle into two adjacent stitches on the left needle and purl them together (Fig. 24).

Fig. 24

Make 1 (M1) is an instruction often seen in patterns. This is a type of increase. On either the knit or purl side, lift the running thread located between the stitches on left and right needles onto the point of the left needle by inserting the needle from front to back. Knit or purl the new stitch in the back (Fig. 25). This stitch will be twisted. This twist prevents a hole from forming below the stitch.

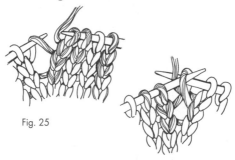

Fig. 25

Kirstin Muench
Muench Yarns, Inc.
muenchyarns.com

I use the cable and long-tail cast-on row for casting on. Remember that you do not count the first V that belongs to the cast-on row.

> Linda Lum DeBono
> lindalumdebono.com

Weave in your ends as you go, so you don't have to face all the sewing in at once. This is especially true when you are using multiple colors in a project.

> Diana McKay and Leslie Taylor
> Mountain Colors, Inc.
> Corvallis, Montana
> mountaincolors.com

Duplicate stitch is a form of embroidery that is unique to knitting. It is worked over stockinette stitch using a tapestry needle and a yarn of the same type and thickness as the fabric. If the yarn is too much thinner it will sink into the knitted stitches, and a thicker yarn could stretch the fabric. Small skeins of embroidery or needlepoint yarns are suitable as long as you use the number of strands that will match the knitting yarn weight. Generally, you will work from a graph, keeping in mind that knit stitches are wider than they are tall.

If your pattern doesn't include a chart for the duplicate stitch, you can make your own and add designs or alphabets to any knit project (Fig. 26). Be sure to use knitter's graph paper, which has rectangular squares. This is available at your local yarn shop or online ready to download.

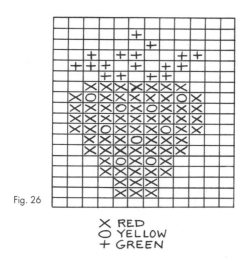

Fig. 26

X RED
O YELLOW
+ GREEN

Duplicate stitches can be worked horizontally, vertically, or diagonally. Be careful to match the embroidery tension to the knitting so there is no puckering. To make horizontal stitches, thread a tapestry needle with an 18-inch length of yarn.

1. Secure the yarn on the wrong side of the fabric and bring the needle through to the front at the base of the first stitch.

2. Insert the needle into the right-hand side of the top of the same stitch, carry the needle and yarn across the back of the work, and bring them to the front on the left side of the same stitch (Fig. 27). Reinsert the needle into the base of the first stitch.

3. Bring the needle up through the base of the stitch to the left of the stitch just duplicated. Repeat step 2.

4. To work the next horizontal, insert the needle into the base of the last horizontal stitch worked and then bring needle and yarn out to the front through the center of that stitch. Turn the work (the design will be upside down) and work horizontal stitches across the second row of pattern stitches, working the same as the previous row. Continue working horizontal stitches right to left on each row.

    For vertical stitches, begin at the lowest point and work upward. Work the same way as for horizontal duplicate

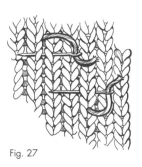

Fig. 27

62

stitch, but bring the needle out to the front through the center of the stitch above the one just worked rather than the stitch to the left (Fig. 28).

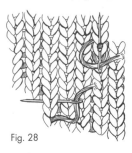

Fig. 28

There are times when you might want to pick up stitches along the edge of a woven fabric. To join knitting to fabric, embroider a row of even chain stitches along the seam line of the fabric. With your knitting needle, pick up a stitch beneath both threads of each chain stitch (Fig. 29), pulling the knit stitch through without going through the fabric. This results in evenly spaced knitting, and as a bonus, the fabric seam allowance will fold back to the wrong side.

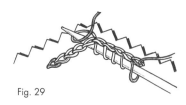

Fig. 29

The three-needle bind-off is a method of binding off and joining two pieces of knitting at the same time. This results in a flat, flexible seam and eliminates the bulk of seaming. It works very well for joining shoulder seams. Here's how.

1. Hold the two pieces to be joined with right sides together. The two needles should be next to each other, pointing in the same direction.

2. Use a third needle (same size) to knit together one stitch from the back needle and one from the front, slipping the finished stitch onto the third needle (Fig. 30). Repeat a second time.

3. Pass the first stitch on the working needle over the second to bind it off.

4. Repeat steps 2 and 3 until all the stitches are bound off. Cut the yarn and pull it through the last stitch on the working needle.

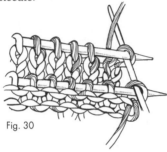

Fig. 30

Weave in the ends so they are invisible from the right side. If there is no seam allowance to weave the ends into, weave the tail into the fabric, matching the direction the yarn was coming from to prevent a hole from forming (Fig. 31). Weave into solid areas, not openwork. Weave diagonally if that is more invisible. If you're working with multiple tails near the same spot, weave them in different directions so the fabric doesn't get too thick in one place. Weave over and under a few stitches, pull the tail snug, then stretch the fabric so the weaving remains elastic.

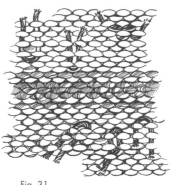

Fig. 31

Are you a picker or a thrower? Most Americans are throwers, using the English style of knitting and throwing the yarn around the left-hand needle with the right hand. Pickers use the continental style of knitting, in which the yarn is picked up by the right needle and pulled through the old stitch. Every English-style knitter should learn continental-style knitting. For one thing, it's faster and can be less stressful to hands and wrists. This is not to say you should give up English style; it's good to have both in your arsenal. Google "continental knitting video," and you'll have quite a few videos to view. Check with your knit shop to see whether a class is offered. There are other styles of knitting as well; Portuguese and Norwegian purl are just two of many other styles. The end result is the same. The differences are in how the yarn is held and tension provided.

How to knit continental style:

1. Hold both the yarn and the needle in your left hand. The trick is to keep the yarn taut. Wind the yarn around your left little finger and over your left forefinger (Fig. 32). Your forefinger should be close to the tip of the left-hand needle. The yarn between the needle and your forefinger should be a bit taut.

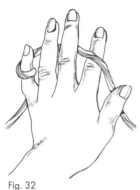

Fig. 32

2. Insert the right-hand needle through the stitch on the left-hand needle. Insert from left to right and front to back (Fig. 33).

3. Swivel the tip of the right-hand needle to the right and under the yarn, scooping up the yarn from your left forefinger (Fig. 34).

Fig. 33

67

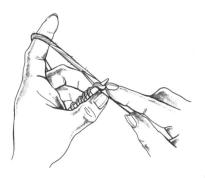

Fig. 34

4.   Pull the yarn through the loop (Fig. 35).

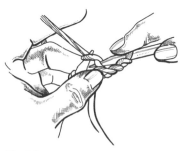

Fig. 35

5.   Slide the old loop off the left-hand needle and let it drop (Fig. 36). Congratulations, you've completed the stitch.

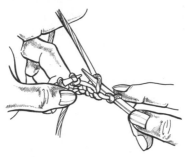

Fig. 36

6. Repeat steps 2 through 5 to continue across the row (Fig. 37). You're now a continental-style knitter.

Fig. 37

The basic chain cast-off technique serves most knitting well, but it can give even better results when you consider the following tips:

- **Cast off with a relaxed** but even tension. If you have difficulty keeping your tension even, try using a needle that is one or two sizes larger than your working needle to ensure a relaxed but even tension.
- **Always cast off in pattern,** knitting the knit stitches and purling the purl stitches.
- **Be generous to yourself** by leaving a long tail of 10 to 12 inches for darning in ends and sewing seams. Scrimping here just makes later tasks a little more difficult.
- **Casting off takes more yarn** than a single row of knitting. If you are nearing the end of your supply of yarn, leave four times the width of one row for the cast-off edge.
- **For a smooth edge,** cast off garter stitch and stockinette stitch from the wrong side.
- **Avoid decreases and increases** in the cast-off row, if possible. For a smoother edge, make these changes one or two rows before the cast-off row. But there are always exceptions.
- **For a sharp square corner,** knit the last two stitches together and then cast off. Chain cast off moves each stitch to the left, leaving you with an angled corner at the last stitch. Knitting the last two stitches together neatly finishes off the edge in line with the selvage and neatly finishes off the edges of scarves, afghan squares, blankets, and the like.

- **If you can't avoid the increases or decreases,** make them evenly across the row.

joining yarns

joining yarns

joining yarns

Knitting warms my heart and soothes my soul.
— Anonymous

Changing to a New Ball of Yarn

1. As you are approaching the end of your working yarn, you can knit a couple of stitches with old yarn.

2. Then take the old yarn and new yarn and knit with them together as if they are one yarn.

3. Knit a couple of stitches with the two yarns held together.

4. Now drop the old yarn and then knit with the new ball of yarn and finish your row as normal.

5. You can come back later and weave in the last little strands of the end of the old yarn and the beginning of

the new yarn. They should disappear into the wrong side of the fabric once they have been washed. Watch a video of this tip at our Web site.

Jimmy Beans Wool
JimmyBeansWool.com

Spit joins are a bit of magic! When working with yarns spun from animal fibers (e.g., wool, mohair, alpaca, cashmere), a spit join is a smooth way to join a new skein. When joining animal fiber yarns of the same color, fray the front end of the new skein and the tail of the previous one, for about 2 inches. Moisten your palm well (spit works great) and overlap the frayed ends in your palm (Fig. 38). Now vigorously rub your palms together, back and forth. Voilà! The frayed ends will felt together, leaving a single, fused strand. No knots or loose ends!

Fig. 38

The join can also be made by moistening your palm and making sure the frayed ends are wet. Twist the overlapped ends until they are well felted (Fig. 39).

Fig. 39

Kay Mather
Rare Purls
Rarepurls.net

Russian join: This is a really slick way to join two yarns together. It works well on any type of yarn.

1. Take the tail end of your old working yarn and the beginning of your new yarn and lay one over the other, so that they cross in the middle. You may want to work on your lap or on a table.

2. Thread the tail end of the old yarn with a tapestry needle and then insert the needle about 1 inch into the length of the old yarn.

3. Pull the needle through until the tail comes out, take the tapestry needle out, and pull the yarn snug, and you have joined the two together on one side.

4. Now we do the exact same thing with the new yarn that you are joining.

5. Then snip the ends, maybe leaving a tiny tail so after your item is washed you can finish the tail up.

You're going to love this join! Watch a video at our Web site.

Jimmy Beans Wool
JimmyBeansWool.com

fit just right

fit just right

When looking for a pattern size, be sure to read "finished bust size" and not just size. Some patterns don't include the ease that you would like or need.

Barry Klein
Trendsetter Yarns
trendsetteryarns.com

. . . .

Know your own measurements, lots of them, not just bust, waist, and hip. Know how long your arms are from wrist to armpit, how long you are from wrist to wrist (arm span) and from neck to waist, how big around your wrists are, and your neck and your foot length, and I'm sure there are more. Knowing these measurements will help you customize the fit of garments. You don't have to have sleeves that are too short or long or cuffs that are too loose or tight.

Remember this when measuring a sweater that is still on the needles. When you bind it off, it will often be a little wider and a little shorter than it seemed to be while on the needles. Allow for this! Sometimes, if precise measurements are important, before binding off I will put the stitches onto a piece of scrap yarn and measure that way before binding off.

Betty Balcomb
Bi Coastal Betty at Ravelry.com

Choosing a size: Many of us are ready to cast on for a new fall sweater. Before a single stitch is knit, you have to determine what size you'll make. Some knitters find this an anxiety-inducing task that entails a lot of guesswork, but with a bit of pattern studying, you'll be able to easily choose your perfect size. Berroco patterns list the exact finished bust measurement at the beginning of the instructions and on the schematic. This puts the power in your hands; you can decide how you would like that sweater to fit. These tips will have you well on your way to a perfectly fitting garment.

1. First, find your bust measurement. Note that this is not your bra band size; instead, measure at the fullest point of your chest.

2. Decide how much ease you would like. The difference between your bust measurement and the finished garment is called ease. Some sweaters will look better with little or no ease, such as lace patterns, ribbed sweaters, or anything meant to be body conscious. Others should have a bit more ease, such as slouchy, comfortable sweaters that are meant to be layered and anything in a bulky yarn. If a style is meant to be oversized, we note it near the size descriptions.

3. If you're not sure how much ease you like, find a piece of clothing you already own that you enjoy the fit of and measure that for a good starting point. It's a great way to find your ideal sleeve and body length, too.

Berroco, Inc.
berroco.com

....

Some sweaters will benefit from shoulder pads to add shape and definition. Commercial pads of foam or batting are generally too stiff for a soft sweater. The solution? Knit your own, and they are quick and easy to make. From the same sweater yarn, knit a square 5 to 6 inches wide using garter stitch (knit every row) for thickness. Fold the square diagonally and overcast the edges together using the yarn end (Fig. 40). Try on the garment and place the pad at the shoulder with the pointed side facing the neck and the folded edge along the edge of the shoulder line. Pin in place and then tack to the sweater with loose stitches at each corner.

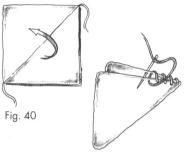

Fig. 40

Review the schematic drawings (Fig. 41) that are part of most garment instructions before you begin. Listed along the edges are the dimensions of the piece in each size. This is a big help in determining the size you'll choose and deciding whether you'll want to make changes for a better fit. The drawing also shows you the shapes of the main pieces.

Fig. 41

BACK AND FRONT

7(7½)
20(21½)
12 (13½)
16 ½ (18 ½)

some really good ideas

some really good ideas

Blocking is often key to making projects look handmade rather than homemade. Take the time to block pieces before joining and to block single-piece projects. It is the difference between "I am through" and "It is finished!"

Kay Mather
Rare Purls
rarepurls.net

. . . .

I changed my blocking habits after a chance remark from Jared Flood. Instead of slipping blocking wires through edge stitches, weave wires over and under two bars between stitch 1 and stitch 2. No more little loopies.

Kit Huchin
Churchmouse Yarns & Teas
Bainbridge Island, Washington
churchmouseyarns.com

Always buy an extra skein of yarn. Just imagine running out! It is worth every penny because you knit with love, whether it's for yourself or as a gift. You always want to have enough yarn.

When knitting a garment, see how far one skein of yarn goes. Look to see what you have left to make sure you have enough.

Save your patterns in a book. Keep your gauge and a yarn label attached to the pattern so you always have reference for future knitting projects. Make sure to take pictures of the finished piece for your memory albums as well.

Barry Klein
Trendsetter Yarns
trendsetteryarns.com

Read your pattern all the way through before you pick up your needles. This way, you know what to expect as you work forward.

Maripat Repach
Royal Palm Beach, Florida

We recommend that you stop knitting after the third glass of wine.

Danielle Romanetti
fibre space
fibrespace.com

Always have at least three projects going at once:

Challenging: If you find yourself in a peaceful and distraction-free environment, you can revel in the magic of lace, cables, or colorwork and thank all the people before you who have helped pass on this wonderful craft.

Interesting: If you are at the doctor's office or waiting for your kids to finish their piano lessons, that's where beautiful handspun can come in handy. It's a simple pattern, but the yarn does all the work. It's like watching a movie!

Mindless: Watching a movie, chatting with friends, listening to lectures or staff meetings—any time you know you can pay better attention if you can keep your hands busy. (This is different from reading the paper while someone is trying to tell you about his or her day.)

Cathy Woodcock
Lantern Moon
lanternmoon.com

In a pinch, you can use a paper clip for a stitch holder.

Becky Keyes
Keepsake Quilting
keepsakequilting.com

Keep a record of all your knitting projects in a three-ring binder with plastic sleeves. For each project, include a copy of the directions (write any comments on this sheet, including changes you have made), a label from your yarn, and a yard or two of the yarn. Take a picture of the finished piece and include that in the sleeve, too.

If you don't like working from charts (or don't feel comfortable using them), you can always write out the instructions line by line. Then, while you work the pattern, you can just check off each row as you go.

Amy Steidl Olson
Keepsake Quilting
keepsakequilting.com

If you don't enjoy knitting two socks at a time on the same needle, try buying two sets of needles, either double pointed or circular, and working both socks together. Knit the top of one, and then do the same on the other. Work the heel flap and turn the heel on one and repeat on the other. If you work in this manner, you will have completed both socks and maybe won't run into the "one-sock syndrome."

Winnie Soester
Colorado Fiber Arts
Pueblo, Colorado
coloradofiberarts.com

Keeping track of rows without a pencil or row counter: Do you ever forget to write down the row you just finished or forget to advance your row counter? Here is an easy method to keep track of your rows. You can't forget because you will need to do something with the marker when you get to it; you just move it to the next loop on right side rows.

1. Take a strand of yarn and loop it in half. Tie as many knots as there are rows in the pattern. Fig. 42 indicates three loops that can be used to keep track of when to make an increase that might need to be made every sixth row.

2. For the first row of flat knitting you will put the needle through the first loop of the yarn marker. When you work the next right-side row you will move the needle into the second loop, indicating you are starting the third row. When you start the next right-side row, you put the needle through the third loop (indicating you are starting the fifth row (Fig. 43). On the next right-side row you will put the needle through the first loop again (indicating you have finished six rows and need to do your increase). You will continue in this manner until all your increases are made. If you need to make your increases every eight, ten, or more rows, just make more loops.

Fig. 42

Fig. 43

Take an occasional count of your stitches. Stitch count is one of the best ways to know that your project is going smoothly. Another way to avoid pattern woes is to visually check your work often. It will sharpen your eye, making you better at reading your knitting, and you can check for problems such as misaligned lace patterns or dropped stitches.

Though some knitters enjoy a glass of wine as they knit, tipsy knitting should be limited to easy yarnie fodder, such as fields of stockinette or garter. And remember, friends do not let friends knit drunk!

Kay Mather
Rare Purls
rarepurls.net

· ·

My best piece of knitting advice I give to my customers is: No matter what the pattern instructs, always do your increasing and decreasing, at least one or two stitches in from the edge, to provide a selvage for finishing.

Candice E. Powell
Yarntiques
Johnson City, Tennessee
yarntiques.com

· ·

Remember when knitting needles weren't allowed on airplanes? I fly for business as well as leisure, and I knew I couldn't get on a plane if I couldn't knit, so I made a plan, and it worked, and I fly domestic and international flights and never not knit.

I know I have your interest, so here's my idea in case it happens again and you have to fly. I wear my hair in a bob that is just below my chin, and I have a set of Denise interchangeable knitting needles, so since I was knitting a shawl with size 7 needles, I put the needles on the circular cable and threaded it through my hair, so I had an ornamental headband. After takeoff, when everyone had settled down I simply took the cable headband out of my hair and knit for the whole flight, and nobody said a word.

Just in case the cable and needles were confiscated, I had a second plan. I carefully researched what would be the smoothest automatic pencils and found a package of six Winnie-the-Pooh plastic pencils with the smoothest join. I snapped off the plastic clip and removed the lead, and these pencils were equal to a size 7 knitting needle. Using lace-weight yarn, I could get as many as 130 stitches on the needle and knit a lace-weight clapotis. I also bought a package of Mickey and Minnie pencils that were like the Winnie-the-Pooh except they were equal to a size 10 knitting needle.

I always have a few packages of the pencils in my bag and a few balls of lace-weight yarn and also fingering-weight yarn, and no matter what the rules are I can zone out listening to my iPod while sitting and knitting on the planes.

> Mary H. Arnold
> Conjoined Creations, LLC
> "Colors with Attitude"
> Cave Creek, Arizona
> conjoinedcreations.com

. . . .

It is very important to understand the distinction of right and wrong versus front and back. When I was a new knitter this always had me very confused.

> Ann Kelliher
> Fancie Purls
> Plymouth, Massachusetts
> fanciepurls.vpweb.com

. . . .

Don't be afraid to knit something really simple. Often, we get too swept up by the pressure to knit something elaborate with shaping and cables and short rows and various adornments. Sometimes it is best to just relax and let stockinettete or garter stitch form underneath the needles and let the yarn do the work for you. Case in point: I made a pair of socks recently with self-striping yarn. The cuff had a moderately elaborate pattern that looked great, but the striping disappeared into the pattern. The foot was just stockinettette, and the stripes emerged in all their glory, and I really like the foot of these socks better than the cuff, and I could have saved an hour or two of my life.

Anytime you are working on a project that looks the same on the back and the front (e.g., garter stitch, most ribbing, seed stitch, checkered patterns), tie a bow or attach a big pin to the right side so you don't have to keep figuring out which is the front and which is the back. I have saved the sanity of quite a few knitters with this tip. Speaking of back and front or wrong side right side, I always love it when I come across the terms "public side" and "private side."

Always leave nice long tails when casting on and binding off while knitting sweaters. Use the tails for sewing up and weave them in as you finish each seam. This results in way fewer ends to weave in, and weaving in fewer ends is always a good thing. At least two of the tails can be used for fixing the pesky holes that seem to end up in the armpits and then just weave them right into one of the several seams that are right there. If you always start new balls of yarn at the edges, the tails can be woven into the seams, an easier weave, and it will never show through to the right side.

I frequently tell the participants in my classes and workshops to never stop in the middle of a row, especially when working lace. Of course, sometimes you have to stop in the middle of a row. It may seem elementary to many of you, but quite a few people aren't sure which direction to start back in when they put down their knitting mid-row. Here's how to get it right every time. Pick up your knitting and look for the working yarn. The needle with the working yarn needs to be in your right hand, and the one without needs to be in your left hand. That's all there is to it.

Betty Balcomb
Bi Coastal Betty at Ravelry.com

. . . .

Whatever you're knitting, remember to include a small note that tells the giftee a bit about the fiber. I like to tell them why I thought they'd like a particular fiber and how to care for it. Never miss a chance to spread a little yarn love!

Berroco, Inc.
berroco.com

. . . .

When it gets late and you are tired, put your knitting down. This is a time when even good knitters can make mistakes. Don't wake up to an "OMG, what have I done?!" moment.

Kay Mather
Rare Purls, Inc.
rarepurls.com

When knitting with unspun roving that comes off the cake from the outside, place the cake on the floor so the yarn has no tension on it and won't pull apart.

John Little
Briggs and Little
briggsandlittle.com

Here's an easy trick to keep track of where you are in a pattern. Place a marker on your working needle before every pattern repeat. Slip the markers as you work. If you make a mistake, it's simple to check each repeat and find the error (Fig. 44).

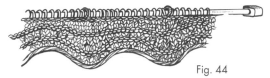

Fig. 44

Maureen Lukenbill
Delray Beach, Florida

Keep a journal of your projects, including where you bought the yarn and a label from one of the skeins just in case you need more later.

When gifting a knitted item, be sure to include a skein label (for proper care instructions) and even a partial skein, if possible, in case repairs are needed later.

Kirstin Muench
Muench Yarns, Inc.
muenchyarns.com

Put one of the rubber or plastic point protectors on the tips of the small scissors you keep in your knitting bag. If the scissors came with a case, use it instead. This protects the points of your scissors and keeps you from getting stabbed when you're reaching into your bag.

A sure way to ensure that both front sides of a cardigan sweater end up exactly the same length is to knit both sides at the same time using two balls of yarn. Cast on for the first side, drop the yarn, and using a second ball of yarn, cast on for the second side. Keep the two yarns from tangling by dropping each into a separate heavy bowl on the floor. You'll need to follow the directions carefully because you'll be reversing for the second side. The upside is that when you've finished you have both sides completed, one step closer to following the no-unfinished-objects rule.

It's very important to keep track of where you are when you're working from a chart. One simple way is to place a sticky note directly below the row you're working. It's easy to pick up and move as you work along. A magnetic board and strip set also works well. Just place your pattern on top of the board, place the strip directly below the working row, and move as needed.

If you share your house with shedding dogs and cats, here's an easy way to keep your work in progress fur free. Lay a thin towel across your lap when you're knitting. When you need to lay your work down, fold the ends of the towel over your work and move.

There are many great circular needle storage items on the market today, but you can also make your own. Buy heavy-duty sheet protectors from your stationery store (Fig. 45). The sheets are closed on three sides and open at the top. They have a strip on the side with holes for placing in a binder. Label the sheet with the needle size and length, and you have your collection at your fingertips.

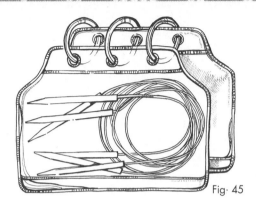

Fig· 45

Another simple way to store those pesky circular needles is in zippered plastic freezer bags. Label each bag with the needle size and length. File in numerical order in a box.

Often we have problems with our work slipping off the needles. One way to eliminate this is to match the yarn fiber to the type of needle. Fibers such as silk and bamboo tend to be more slippery than wool and cotton. If you're having problems, try matching silk yarn to bamboo needles and rougher wool yarns to metal needles.

If you are knitting a large or heavy garment without any support underneath, your stitches can slip off the needles, and this can also cause wrist and arm strain. Avoid these problems by laying the garment in your lap or on a table in front of you.

If you use circular needles, simply turn the needle ends toward the center of your work and run them through the fabric. Your knitting won't slip off the needles.

Use a snap-top eyeglass case to carry double-pointed needles in your knitting bag. This will protect them from an accidental break.

let's get organized

let's get organized

Properly practiced, knitting soothes the troubled spirit, and it doesn't hurt the untroubled spirit either.
—Elizabeth Zimmerman

Because I'm an organizer of all things, probably the most important thing for me is to have all the tools I need for any project I am working on. When I begin a project, I assemble everything I need first. I have multiple small zipped bags that contain thread cutter or scissors, measuring tape or small ruler, pencil, sticky notes, stitch markers, small crochet hook, and tapestry needle. Each project bag gets started with one of these startup kits of tools, the pattern in a clear document holder, the yarn, and all needles needed. Then I'm ready to get started!

Penny Sitler
Executive Director, The Knitting Guild Association
TKGA.com

Store your knitting needles in a worm binder. These are normally used by fishermen to organize their fishing lures. It has a number of thick plastic sleeves that keep everything organized and a hard shell that folds out to be a stable surface when you are traveling. It is indispensable for storing knitting needles by size. The worm binders come in all sizes, from small to jumbo.

Storage space can be a problem for many of us. It's not necessary to keep every issue of every magazine you receive. Photocopy or cut out the patterns and articles that you want to keep and slip each one into its own lightweight clear plastic sheet protector. Place in a three-ring binder using dividers to separate them into cardigans, scarves, baby items, and so on. Before you know it you'll have a personal collection of potential projects. For the pack rats among us, there are jumbo binders available, and you don't have to stop at one binder.

mistakes and the good fix

mistakes and the good fix

For you created my inmost being,
You knit me together in my mother's womb.
—Psalm 139:13

People regularly ask me how I learned to fix mistakes. I can fix mistakes because I can read the fabric and see immediately what was done wrong. Learn to read your fabric. Watch yourself knitting. Understand why a knit stitch looks like a little heart and a purl stitch looks like a bump. It's because of the way you are flipping the stitch on the needle over the strand of yarn. Knit flips back with strand behind work, purl flips forward with strand in front of work. When you get this, you will have a much easier time spotting and then fixing mistakes. Go to the spot where the stitch is wrong, orient the stitch and yarn so you can create a knit or purl stitch, and make it look like the stitch it was meant to be.

Errors in previous rows happened to me this week: I did a purl stitch instead of a knit stitch. I knit to where the stitch occurs and stop at the top of the column. I let go or undo the stitches down to the row where the error happened and redo the stitch. I like to use a crochet hook to hook the stitches back up to the top again. If you need to fix a K stitch, start your crochet hook from the front of the piece and hook. If you need to fix a P stitch, start your crochet hook from the back of the piece and hook.

Linda Lum DeBono
lindalumdebono.com

Dropped stitches can be fixed. If the stitch was dropped several rows below the one you are working on, a ladder will have formed. Use a crochet hook to work the dropped stitch up the ladder rung by rung. To fix a knit stitch, insert the hook into the stitch from the front (Fig. 46). To fix a purl stitch, insert the hook into the stitch from the back (Fig. 47). When you reach the top row, position the stitch on the left needle, making sure not to twist this stitch.

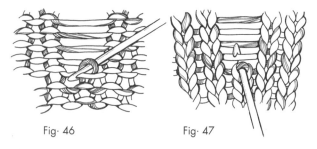

Fig. 46   Fig. 47

Tinking and lurping. When you've made a mistake and need to unknit stitches, that's called tinking (with knit spelled backwards); likewise, unpurling is called lurping. Okay, it's silly, but it explains what you're doing.

Sometimes you need to rip back a good many rows. To speed up the process, use a needle several sizes smaller than the working needles. Run it under the front leg of every stitch on the row below the mistake (Fig. 48). Then, just rip away. The ripping stops when you get to the thin needle and all the stitches are turned correctly. Slip the stitches onto the working needle and knit away.

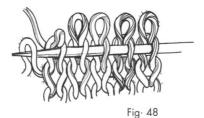

Fig. 48

knitting abbreviations

knitting abbreviations

I'm a lean, mean knitting machine.
—Anonymous

The following is a list of knitting abbreviations used by yarn industry designers and publishers.

[ ]	work instructions within brackets as many times as directed
( )	work instructions within parentheses in the place directed
* *	repeat instructions following the asterisks as directed
˝	inches

beg	begin or beginning
BO	bind off
CA	color A
CB	color B
CC	contrasting color
cm	centimeters
cn	cable needle
CO	cast on
cont	continue
dec	decrease, decreases, or decreasing
dpn	double-pointed needle(s)
fl	front loop(s)
inc	increase, increases, or increasing
k or K	knit

k2tog	knit two stitches together
kwise	knitwise
LH	left hand
M1	make one stitch
MC	main color
p or P	purl
pat(s)	pattern(s)
pm	place marker
p2tog	purl two stitches together
p2so	pass two stitches over
p2sso	pass two slipped stitches over
psso	pass slipped stitch over
pwise	purlwise
rem	remain or remaining

rep	repeat(s)
rev St st	reverse stockinette stitch
RH	right hand
rnd(s)	round(s)
RS	right side
sk	skip
skp	slip, knit, pass stitch over; one stitch decrease
sl	slip
sl1k	slip one knitwise
sl1p	slip one purlwise
sl st	slip stitch(es)
ssk	slip, slip, knit two stitches together, a decrease
st(s)	stitch(es)

St st	stockinette stitch
tbl	through back loop(s)
tog	together
WS	wrong side
wyib	with yarn in back
wyif	with yarn in front
yfwd	yarn forward
yo	yarn over

we all could use
some inspiration

we all could use some inspiration

Knit on, with confidence and hope,
through all crises.
— Elizabeth Zimmerman

Play with colors and textures that you may not be ready for. You may be very pleasantly surprised. Ask some friends over for an evening of knitting. Everyone brings 10 to 15 skeins of yarn from their stash and a stitch book. Sit around and play with yarns in a variety of stitches, mixing up your normal selections with things that are different. Try new stitches and think outside the box.

Barry Klein
Trendsetter Yarns
trendsetteryarns.com

When I first started knitting I looked everywhere for motifs with which to experiment and was often inspired by old quilt blocks.

Kaffe Fassett
Kaffe Fassett Design
kaffefassett.com

. . . .

Nothing is hard unless you think it is. Try everything. You may surprise yourself!

Kate Gilbert
Twist Collective
twistcollective.com

. . . .

Be the boss of your knitting. If you like the look of the wrong side of a stitch pattern better, use it on the public or right side. If you want to use another yarn, try it. If you like trim, add it. It is your project, and you are the boss.

Kay Mather
Rare Purls
rarepurls.net

. . . .

I just put stuff together until they sing; if not, I try some other combination.

Kaffe Fassett
Kaffe Fassett Design
kaffefassett.com

I'm fairly new to the knitting world and quite basic in my approach to technique. In the process of learning to knit I realized that the cables, fancy stitches, and unusual shapes would distract from the impact I wanted to create. So I concentrated on using good old stocking stitch and the fabulous intarsia and Fair Isle techniques that enable you to control color changes and knit in your ends as you work. Take advantage of all the yarns you have available, and if they are not on your doorstep look a little further, remembering that there is always the Internet and mail order.

Brandon Mably
Brandon Mably Designs
brandonmably.com

. . . .

My best tip I give when teaching is that there isn't a right and a wrong way. If it works, great!

Jennifer Orr
Alpaca with a Twist & Copper Ridge Alpacas
AlpacaWithATwist.com

. . . .

Start a knitting library of your very own. Start with a good encyclopedia of knitting stitches (one of Barbara Walker's *Treasury of Knitting Patterns* books is a good choice) and a basic "how to knit" book. Then add Elizabeth Zimmerman's *Knitting*

Without Tears or *The Opinionated Knitter*. There are specialty stitch books available, such as ones featuring only lace stitches or textured stitches. Browse your library, local yarn shop, local bookstores, and online stores to find just the right books for you. You don't need a large collection, just the basics. But it is fun to add one when you find a title that says, "You need me!"

Subscribe to a knitting magazine. There are so many available today. Go to your local yarn shop, library, and bookstore to browse through their collections to find one or two that speak to you. Then sign up. It's fun to anticipate that next issue.

Join a knitting guild if one is in your area. Find out by going to www.TKGA.org or check with your local yarn shop. If several of your acquaintances enjoy knitting, start an informal knitting group meeting at each other's homes. There are probably knitters in every group you're associated with, all potential knitting group members. The camaraderie is a wonderful thing.

Many yarn shops have a knitting table where customers can gather at a specific date and time. And almost every shop offers a wide variety of classes, and many offer private lessons. Take a class and learn something new. Knitting classes are often included in school board adult education courses.

Sometimes we hit a stumbling block. Your local yarn shop can help you out. However, please have the courtesy not to ask for help when you did not purchase the materials from them.

And there are even more opportunities for knitting adventure, such as countless retreats (check with your local yarn shop and the Internet), knitting cruises, overseas travel that is fiber related, and resident schools with short-term programs such as John C. Campbell Folk School and Haystack Mountain School.

Almost every yarn company has a Web site that offers information on their yarns. Many offer newsletters, which are packed with information, and others offer patterns, knitting tips, and videos. A wealth of information is there for the taking. See the list of yarn companies and their Web addresses at the back of this book.

Get involved in a knitting project either as an individual or part of a knitting group. Here are just a few choices – you'll think of many more.

- Preemie hats for your local hospital's neonatal intensive care unit
- Baby blankets for an abused women's shelter
- Helmet liners or socks for overseas troops

- Afghans for your local Veteran's Administration hospital
- Knit items to sell at your church or social club bazaar

How did we get along without the Internet? If you're not computer savvy, learn. It becomes more important with each passing year. The Internet is an endless source of information. Most of us learn visually, and if a picture hasn't made the lesson quite clear enough, you'll find many, many videos online showing you just how it's done. Some videos are quite professional, some are amateurish, but you'll learn from them all. Just Google your subject—let's say intarsia—and you'll be amazed at the information that pops up.

And don't forget the knitting communities on the Internet, such as Ravelry (ravelry.com), Knitting Daily (knittingdaily.com), or many others. An online community is a group of people who interact and share ideas about something they have in common, in this case knitting.

yarn companies and
their web sites

yarn companies and their web sites

Knitting forever, housework whenever.
—Anonymous

Alpaca with a Twist
Alpacawithatwist.com

Artyarns
artyarns.com

Berroco, Inc.
berroco.com

Cascade Yarns
cascadeyarns.com

Classic Elite Yarns
classiceliteyarns.com

Elann.com
elann.com

Knit One, Crochet Too, Inc.
knitonecrochettoo.com

Knit Picks
knitpicks.com

Koigu Wool Designs
koigu.com

Kraemer Yarns
kraemeryarns.com

Lion Brand Yarns
lionbrandyarns.com

Lorna's Laces
lornaslaces.net

Malabrigo Yarn
malabrigoyarn.com

Muench Yarns, Inc.
muenchyarns.com

Patons
patonsyarns.com

Plymouth Yarn Co.
plymouthyarn.com

Prism
prismyarn.com

Skacel Collection, Inc.
skacelknitting.com

Tahki-Stacy Charles, Inc.
Tahkistacycharles.com

Trendsetter Yarns
trendsetteryarns.com

Westminster Fibers
westminsterfibers.com

COLLECT ALL
POCKET POSH® TITLES!